Original title:
Leaf by Leaf

Copyright © 2025 Creative Arts Management OÜ
All rights reserved.

Author: Theodore Sinclair
ISBN HARDBACK: 978-1-80581-818-2
ISBN PAPERBACK: 978-1-80581-345-3
ISBN EBOOK: 978-1-80581-818-2

In the Quiet Shade

Under trees that wear a grin,
Squirrels chatter, let the fun begin.
Rabbits hop in circles neat,
While birds shout, 'Hey, take a seat!'

A branch sways with a silly dance,
A leaf flutters as if in a trance.
Sunbeams flash a playful peek,
Nature's court is just a freak!

The Art of Erosion

Rocks roll down, it's quite absurd,
While old tree trunks just laugh and curd.
Wind whispers jokes, and rivers giggle,
Erosion's art, a funny wiggle!

Soil slips past—oh what a sight!
A dance of dirt, just in the night.
Moss grins wide as it takes a stage,
Nature's humor is all the rage!

A Symphony of Rustling

In the breeze, leaves sing a song,
A cacophony of giggles all day long.
Branches bend and sway with glee,
Nature's symphony, a wild spree!

Crickets join in with a squeaky flair,
While beetles bust out a boogie affair.
Even the acorns roll with cheer,
As laughter echoes far and near!

Heartbeats Beneath the Bark

Underneath where laughter lives,
Quiet critters share their gifts.
Each thump, a joke, a tickling tease,
Stirring giggles in the breeze!

Roots join in, they wiggle around,
Creating giggles underground.
Every beat is a funny spark,
Life's a joke, hiding in the bark!

The Rustle of Distant Dreams

In the breeze, they dance and sway,
Whispering secrets, come what may.
With each flap, they tell a tale,
Of dancing squirrels and a wind-blown gale.

Do you hear the giggles in the air?
As twigs join in this merry affair.
The branches sway, a comedic show,
Underneath, the acorns giggle below.

Silly shadows play on the ground,
As they leap and twist all around.
A butterfly fuels a joyous chase,
While a sneaky raccoon joins the race.

With every rustle, laughter grows,
A silly breeze, anything goes!
In this woodland, joy takes flight,
Where dreams drift softly, day and night.

A Tincture of Gold and Time

Autumn's laugh, a rich delight,
Sprinkles of gold, oh what a sight!
Each twirl and tumble, a playful jest,
Nature's comedy at its best.

The sunbeams weave through every gap,
Tickling fronds, a sunny clap.
While cheeky birds sing silly tunes,
And dance around like cartoon loons.

Oh, what a ruckus, crunching sounds,
As critters plot on ageless grounds.
Gifts of color, nature's prank,
Where laughter weaves in every flank.

Peeking through branches, whispering glee,
As trees share tales of what's to be.
In this mosaic of time and gold,
The funniest stories wait to be told!

Serenade of the Seasons

Spring sneezed and budded, oh what a sight,
Flowers giggled, swaying in delight.
Summer chuckled with its sunlit rays,
Painting the world in warm, jazzy plays.

Autumn winked, tossed its colored flair,
With a whoosh, the leaves danced through the air.
Winter slipped on ice, gave a comical slide,
Snowflakes laughed as they joined in the ride.

Time's Gentle Hand

Time tickled the clock, gave it a shake,
Hours wiggled out like a playful snake.
Minutes bounced round, refusing to rest,
Counting their giggles at a light-hearted jest.

Seconds sneaked in with their sneaky tricks,
Hiding behind clouds like playful little pricks.
Every tick-tock sang a cheeky tune,
While days juggled laughter under the moon.

The Weight of Summer

Summer came barging with a big, goofy grin,
Loading up sunshine like a cranky old tin.
Sweat beads were laughing, round rolling pins,
While popsicles melted, losing their skins.

The beach was a circus, full of splashes and shouts,
With sunscreen fights and sandcastle bouts.
Summer giggled, 'This is my scene!'
As flip-flops flopped like a comical machine.

Dancers in the Sunlight

Sunbeams twirled with a playful flair,
As shadows shuffled all without a care.
The flowers twinkled in a wild ballet,
While buzzing bees made a mad cabaret.

Grasshoppers hopped on their tiny toes,
While butterflies flitted with joyful shows.
The world was a stage, where humor was spun,
In the warm embrace of the bright summer sun.

A Lament for the Dying

Oh plants, oh woes, what did you say?
Your greens are fading day by day!
Who knew a sprinkle of water too late,
Would send you towards that dreadful fate?

The sun smiles bright, yet you look gray,
Is there a party else where you stray?
I seek your company in this room,
Instead, I feel your pending doom!

Sifting Through Seasons

Winter whispers, 'Stop the play!'
While summer shouts, 'Let's dance away!'
Autumn's giggle sends them all flying,
As spring just laughs, 'Keep on trying!'

In every rustle, a secret shared,
Yet all feel puzzled, too unprepared.
The seasons mix, a silly scheme,
Turning every plant to a wild dream!

The Breath of the Forest

In the woods, there's jest and cheer,
Trees are gossiping, lend an ear!
One claims a bird stole its hat,
While another swears it's just a cat!

Moss giggles low, as shadows creep,
A squirrel squeaks, 'You need more sleep!'
Laughter echoes through the tall trunks,
Nature's punchline pokes and shrinks!

Chronicles of a Single Stem

Behold, a stem, so proud and spry,
Telling tales of days gone by!
It dreamt of blooms and jubilant cheer,
But found itself stuck far from here!

It peers at flowers, so bright, so high,
With every breeze, it lets out a sigh.
"I'll grow, I swear!" it boldly claims,
Yet trips on weeds and funny games!

Mapping the Colors of Time

In autumn's grand parade, I see,
The colors dance, wild and free.
A critter laughed as it slipped by,
Waving a twig, it said, 'Oh my!'

The reds and yellows wore a crown,
While squirrels sang, 'Just sit us down!'
A hidden acorn, oh what luck!
The forest chuckled, 'What the cluck?'

With every gust, a funny twist,
The branches sway, can't resist.
A tumble here, a roll from there,
As nature plays its playful dare.

Ephemeral Shades

In the breeze, a shadow flits,
Dancing around with all its wits.
A turtle stares and gives a sigh,
While pondering why it can't fly.

Orange whispers, 'What a spree!'
While purple shouts, 'Don't bother me!'
The colors argue, 'I'm the best!'
Nature laughs and takes a rest.

A snapshot here, a wink right there,
The playful hues fill up the air.
With every shade that bids goodnight,
They tumble, giggling out of sight.

Rustling Secrets of the Forest

Underneath the leafy roof,
Whispers poke and play aloof.
A raccoon hides with snacks in tow,
As secrets from the trees bestow.

The branches gossip, 'Did you hear?'
A squirrel's tale from yesteryear.
The mushrooms chuckle with delight,
As shadows turn to dance at night.

A rustle here, a giggle there,
The forest sings, 'Don't you dare!'
A pine cone plots its cheeky prank,
On woodland critters, words to crank.

Embrace of the Breezes

The breezes tease with ticklish hands,
As they swirl through the leafy lands.
A wind chime sings, 'Come take a ride!'
The giggling gusts won't let me hide.

I chase the breeze, it runs away,
It whispers jokes in a playful way.
Though leaves may flutter and tumble down,
They wear their colors like a crown.

A funny spin, a silly twirl,
While nature plays, and nuts unfurl.
So dance along, let laughter rise,
In this game of wind and skies.

A Tapestry in the Wind

Once a branch threw a party,
Inviting petals and pine cones.
But the winds were quite naughty,
And swept all the snacks to unknowns.

The acorns danced on the grass,
While the squirrels just could not wait.
They nibbled on all that they could,
Till the party turned into a fate.

A butterfly showed up late,
Wings fluttering like a grand show.
She tripped on a leaf and found fate,
Landed right in a popcorn throw.

Now they gather in giggles,
Whispers flutter through the trees.
For the best time is in wiggles,
And nothing's lighter than a breeze.

The Heartbeat of the Grove

In a grove where shadows play,
Each root and branch seeks some fun.
They laugh at the squirrels all day,
As the sunshine begins to run.

An old stump tells tales by night,
Of owls wearing stylish hats.
While fireflies buzz with delight,
They're the dancers, the stars, and the chats.

A squirrel wears a leaf for a cape,
Pretending to be a brave knight.
Each nut that he finds is escape,
From a shadowy world, out of sight.

Here in this folly of cheer,
Even the mushrooms join in the beat.
With a rhythm echoing clear,
Nature's strange but it's oh-so sweet!

Echoes of the Forest Floor

Down where the critters reside,
The mushrooms boast of their size.
But the ants with a secret decide,
To play games beneath the blue skies.

A beetle races with flair,
While the snails plot their slow pace.
Each whisper holds a silly dare,
As nature shapes its own race.

Bark meets bark in a feast,
As trees gossip in a hush.
Every twig has a tale at least,
Branching out with a lively rush.

So if you hear laughter's call,
Join in with the forest's song.
For mirth is hidden in it all,
And the fun keeps on going strong.

The Dance of the Whispering Trees

In a grove where the breezes twirled,
Trees swayed with a giggling song.
They spun tales of a wacky world,
As the winds hummed right along.

With branches all tangled in glee,
They swapped their jokes from afar.
"Why do stars play hide and seek?"
"Because they know just who they are!"

The shadows join with their jive,
Swaying like a puppet show.
Leaves giggle, feeling alive,
In this dance where laughter grows.

So if ever you wander near,
And hear whispers tickle your ear,
Know that the trees share some cheer,
In the shimmer of each passing year.

Threads of Nature's Palette

In the garden, colors bloom,
Some are bright, while others loom.
The carrots wear a shade of green,
While funky flowers make a scene.

Petunias gossip with the bees,
As they dance upon the breeze.
A cabbage in a silly hat,
Claims to know where all's at.

Beneath the sun, they start to play,
Singing songs of a sunny day.
They'll spin and twirl, in garden glee,
A comedy of life, you see!

With paints of red, and strokes of gold,
Nature's canvas, bold and cold.
So let's rejoice, from sprout to stem,
In this art show, we're all in jest!

The Turning of the Seasons

Spring skips in with leaps and bounds,
While winter grumbles 'round and 'round.
Summer sun runs in a race,
As autumn blushes, picks up pace.

Oh, what fun the seasons bring,
From chilly chills to sultry spring.
The snowman wears a funny tie,
While birds in coats laugh as they fly.

Each change is like a circus show,
With weather jokes that steal the show.
The clouds all giggle, swish and sway,
As rainbows wink and dance away.

So here we are, in nature's flip,
On this merry seasonal trip.
Just like a hat that's worn askew,
Life's quirks delight, it's all so new!

Autumn's Lullaby

The leaves collapse like tired troops,
In dance of colors, twirls, and loops.
Pumpkins roll with a squishy laugh,
As squirrels play a cheeky gaffe.

The air grows crisp, with hints of spice,
As children yell, 'Let's roll the dice!'
With apple cider, warm and sweet,
Nature's snack - a tasty treat!

Tipped hats and boots, all stamp around,
As hoots and howls of joy abound.
The trees tell tales of once green life,
Now sprinkled gold, a painter's knife.

So snuggle close, in blankets tight,
And giggle at the chilly night.
With laughter shared, let's sing and sway,
Autumn's song will lead the way!

Fluttering Sagas

A butterfly with stuffy nose,
Dances lightly as it goes.
It flutters by with a little spin,
Saying, 'Oh, what a dizzy win!'

Bees are buzzing, each with flair,
They argue who's the best in air.
With pollen cakes and nectar sips,
They soar about with silly flips.

The ladybugs in dotty hues,
Swirl around in playful blues.
They gossip 'neath the dappled sun,
In their world, all's funny fun.

So watch the skies as stories weave,
In nature's play, it's hard to leave.
Each flutter brings a laugh, a cheer,
In this saga, joy is near!

The Poetry of Decay

Once a vibrant, green delight,
Now crisp and brown, what a sight!
They flutter down, like jokes quite lame,
Nature's way of playing a game.

Crinkled faces, a fluttery dance,
In the wind, they take a chance.
Twirling down with a giggle and spin,
A farewell party, oh where to begin!

With each plop on the ground, a new tale,
Tattling secrets of storms and hail.
The carpet below, a patchwork of cheer,
Who knew that decay could bring such a beer?

A ballet of dust, in a gusty whiff,
Nature serves up its comic gift.
So here's to the fun, as they fall one by one,
In the grand comedy, they are never outdone.

A Journey Through Verdant Dreams

In the garden, the antics unfold,
Petals whisper secrets, bold.
Chasing shadows, away they flee,
On a quest for the tallest tree.

Swaying, swaying, the branches tease,
Laughing lightly in the breeze.
What wonders lie in the dusk so deep?
The rustling leaves hold dreams in keep.

A snail in a hurry, it seems so odd,
While a worm croons softly, a serenade, quite flawed.
Together they plot, a parade from the bed,
To crown a great king, with a hat made of bread.

In the twilight, as colors swirl,
The critters engage in a wacky whirl.
With each mischief, the night takes form,
In this dreamland, silliness is the norm.

Colors of a Waning Day

As the sun dips low, hues start to fade,
Orange giggles haunt the glade.
A splash of purple, a wink from blue,
Silly skies, what mischief they brew!

Twilight stretches, yawning wide,
Colors clash like a jovial ride.
A burst of laughter fills the air,
While shadows creep, unaware of the flare.

Beneath the trees, critters play dodge,
Rabbits race under the hedge, quite a sodge.
Whiskers twitch, as they plot their prank,
Under the draping, chaotic plank.

The day concedes to the night's merry hum,
In the twilight glow, all voices become.
Every hue that faded sparked a laugh,
In this colorful chaos, they find their path.

Trees in Twilight's Reflection

Oh, the trees with their gnarled hands,
Contemplating over forgotten lands.
In twilight's dance, they twist and twirl,
Shadows pulling a prank, watch them whirl!

They gossip softly, leaves whispering fun,
Nocturnal antics have just begun.
Branches shake with a chuckle, quite bold,
In this twilight play, no secrets are told.

A raccoon strums on a leafy guitar,
While owls hoot jokes from the nearest car.
Each snicker, a rustle, a chorus of glee,
In this evening's theater, all spirits run free!

So as night blankets the forest with cheer,
Harmony reaches not far, nor near.
The trees stand tall, in jest and in song,
In twilight's embrace, they all belong.

The Sway of the Senses

A squirrel leaps, with no care at all,
Chasing shadows, making a call.
The branches bend, they twist and shout,
Who knew nature could be so loud?

In the breeze, a tickle on my nose,
A dance of petals, just like a rose.
The birds squawk jokes, oh what a show,
Nature's comedy, putting on a glow!

Colors collide like paint on a chair,
While bugs adopt a wiggly flair.
What's that aroma? A picnic awaits,
Nature's refreshments, oh, the great plates!

With every rustle, a giggle is heard,
Who knew trees could spread such a word?
So sway with the senses, let laughter unfurl,
In the vibrant, whimsical twirl of this world!

Traces of What Was

Once a crown, now a burnt-out thing,
A crumpled leaf, waiting for spring.
In the corner, a tale is spun,
A crunchy whisper, a giggle of fun.

Here lies the shadow of yesterday's hue,
A memory colored in nature's view.
What happened to brightness? Gone to a friend,
Napping in autumn, it's time to pretend!

A dance with the ghosts of green and gold,
As robins recount all the stories told.
With every tumble, a smile is spread,
Traces of laughter fill up our heads!

So gather those moments, let's giggle and play,
In the remnants of life, come join the fray.
For even what's lost can still be a cheer,
In every crackle, a memory here!

Ebb and Flow of the Seasons

Winter grumbles, "Hey, I'm still here!"
While spring hops in with a reckless cheer.
"Come dance with me" sings the radiant sun,
As snowflakes melt, "Oh boy, this is fun!"

Summer arrives with a popsicle grin,
While autumn laughs, stealing that spin.
"Nature's a circus, watch the show unfold!"
As the leaves play tag, all red, green, and gold.

A toss of a breeze, a tumble of brown,
Everything giggles as seasons spin around.
Let's cha-cha through each, with skips and jumps,
Each turn is a tickle, with joyful thumps!

So waggle your branches and sway with the tide,
In the ebb and flow where no one can hide.
For every season, a party parade,
A wiggle of nature, oh the fun we've made!

Nature's Final Reverie

At dusk, nature chuckles with glee,
As snuggled leaves drift silently.
Crickets hum tales of days gone by,
While the moon laughs, like a twinkling eye.

The branches bow as stars take the stage,
Whispering secrets from history's page.
A last hurrah for the shades of the day,
With a squeaky chorus, they sing and sway!

Laughter echoes from the dimming light,
A playful wisp, a heartwarming sight.
Let's twirl in the twilight, with giggles and sighs,
In nature's reverie, where joy never dies!

So gather the yesterdays, laughter in tow,
As the day bids adieu, we savor the glow.
For nature's a jester, a warm-hearted friend,
In her final delight, the fun has no end!

The Breath of October

October dances with a caper,
Wearing hats made of paper.
The trees chuckle, all aglow,
While squirrels put on quite a show.

Pumpkin spice wafts through the air,
But who forgot to comb their hair?
Costumes hanging in the halls,
While laughter echoes through the walls.

Crunching steps underfoot so loud,
The kids are all feeling quite proud.
Candy corn and goofy smirks,
As autumn laughs and winks, and quirks.

A whispering chill greets the night,
As the moon grins with pure delight.
October's breath, a silly breeze,
Twirling leaves with the greatest of ease.

Harvesting Time's Dreams

Baskets full and spirits high,
The apples jest, they bounce and fly.
Corn cob jokes planted in rows,
Giggling grains as the sunlight glows.

The pumpkins puff up, round and grand,
While farmers dance in the golden sand.
A chicken crossing to join the fun,
Or was it two? Oh, what a run!

Scarecrow chuckles with straw-stuffed pride,
As critters scurry and try to hide.
Witty winds whispering divine,
Harvesting giggles in a straight line.

Mirth and mirth just dancing around,
As harvest dreams tumble to the ground.
With laughter bright, the fields are seen,
A parade of joy, the year's routine.

When the World Holds Its Breath

In the stillness where laughter dies,
The world turns to blink, oh so wise.
A hiccup in time, a chuckle to share,
As pumpkins sneak a little scare.

A cat in shades walks down the street,
With a swagger that can't be beat.
Chasing shadows, oh what a sight,
While birds serenade the October night.

Expecting solemn, we get a grin,
As the breeze mischiefs with a spin.
Every twirl a giggly affair,
Time holds its breath, unplucked, laid bare.

In the stillness, secrets abound,
Laughter hides where joy is found.
When the world waits, the fun unknots,
In the pauses, we tie our thoughts.

Wisps of a Wandering Breeze

A whispering breeze hops to and fro,
Teasing leaves as they come and go.
With wiggles and jiggles, they take flight,
In the twilight, what a delight!

The trees gossip, the wind cracks jokes,
Shaking branches, the laughter provokes.
Chasing acorns on a wild spree,
Squirrelly antics for you and me.

Chasing petals, twirling ahead,
An autumn ballet, in colors spread.
While dandelion dreams gently sway,
The evening chuckles in an airy play.

In a cozy nook, fun takes cheer,
With winks from the night, so crystal clear.
Wandering breezes play tag with us,
In the laughter, life's playful thrust.

Seasons' Final Waltz

As autumn whirls with a quirky flair,
Leaves don costumes, oh what a scare!
A pirouette here, a leap with glee,
Nature's dance, wild as can be.

Squirrels bopping in mismatched socks,
Playing hopscotch on the old brown rocks.
Crispy crunches underfoot galore,
Who knew nature's stage could hold more?

A gust of wind starts a slapstick scene,
Spinning acorns, where have they been?
They tumble and roll in a dizzying cheer,
Each twirl and twist, brings laughter near.

Amidst the chaos, a final bow,
For all the seasons, take a look now.
The curtain drops with a colorful swoosh,
In this grand ballet, there's no need to rush!

Dance of the Dwindling

Tiny dancers twirl on that branch,
Waving goodbye in a comical ranch.
With wobbly moves and laughter loud,
They wiggle and giggle, oh so proud!

In this show of colors fading fast,
The russet and gold take a cheeky cast.
A rustle here, a tumble there,
Such graceful folly fills the air!

With each wobbly drop, a prankster's delight,
Spreading their joy in a fun little fight.
They flutter and flutter, it's quite the spree,
As if they know they're too silly to be!

Then with a whoosh, they spiral down,
To land with a plop right next to the crown.
Silly shivers and shenanigans rear,
In nature's dance, there's nothing to fear!

Shadows Flitting

Shadows play tag in the fading light,
Chasing each other, oh what a sight!
The trees are giggling, they whisper and sway,
Such cheeky antics at the end of the day.

With every flicker, a playful tease,
They dance on the sidewalk as if to please.
Branches are stretching to reach for a star,
While shadows embroider the evening bazaar.

A whispering leaf makes a quick retreat,
Dodging the shadows, it's quite the feat!
They tumble and tumble with a silly grin,
In this lightly skated game of win!

With laughter lingering, night takes the stage,
The playful duet, a colorful page.
Under the stars, a party so grand,
Shadows and whispers take a merry stand!

The Colorful Exodus

A parade of colors starts to unfurl,
In this fruity circus, watch them whirl!
Orange and yellow, a festive sight,
They hop on the breeze, oh what a flight!

The maples giggle, the oaks look sly,
As reds and browns wave a jovial goodbye.
Swaying and swaying, they twirl away,
As if the wind beckons them join the play.

Pinecones cheer, and acorns salute,
To the rhythm of rustling, a jubilant route.
In this zany escape, there's no room for gloom,
Just laughter and joy as they zoom to their doom!

With one last jig on the forest floor,
They scatter in heaps, oh what a chore!
Yet under a smile, they find their way,
In the colorful exodus, they join in the fray!

Memories on a Brisk Wind

Whispers of laughter, crisp in the air,
Stories of squirrels, without a care.
A tumble and roll, what a sight,
Chasing shadows, oh what delight!

Chasing a whiff of pies in the sky,
As clumsy birds stumble, oh my, oh my!
With every gust, a memory flies,
Wink at the past as it zigzags and lies.

Frolic and dance in the autumn chill,
Every gust brings a chuckle, a thrill.
As puffs of fluff shimmy and sway,
In this playful, swirling ballet.

When the sun dips low, and twilight gleams,
Puffing on dreams like sweet candy streams.
Pies, pranks, and polka dots galore,
In this brisk wind, who could ask for more?

Garden Symphony in Orange and Gold

In the garden of giggles, colors ignite,
Pumpkins are blushing, such a funny sight.
Bees buzzing tunes, harmonies sweet,
While scarecrows jiggle, tapping their feet.

The carrots are gossiping, topsy-turvy,
Whispering secrets, a bit too nervy.
With marigolds twisting, putting on shows,
Winking at snails in comical prose.

Tomatoes blushing, caught in a laugh,
As the gardener's tools stage a craft.
Singing with color and silly routine,
In this garden, a bright, laughing scene.

So come join this chorus, where nature's a friend,
In orange and gold, let the giggles extend.
With a merry duet beneath the blue sky,
In this vibrant symphony, let's soar, let's fly!

An Ode to Transience

A tumble of snippets, life's comic strip,
Fleeting moments, on a speedy trip.
The clock's a joker; tick-tock, it teases,
As memories scatter like little breezes.

Bananas that slip, pies that are thrown,
In a blink they're gone, yet still, they've grown.
With chuckles and giggles, on time we rely,
As fleeting as raindrops, or a butterfly.

Quirky decisions, like dressed-up socks,
Or runaway cats that hide in the blocks.
Life's a carnival, vibrant and spry,
Where the fleeting moments just wave goodbye.

So raise up your glass to the ticking parade,
For the funny little quirks that our lives have made.
With a wink and a laugh, let transience sing,
Embrace every foolish and whimsical thing!

Nature's Gentle Farewell

As the sun yawns wide, and colors depart,
The trees shed their giggles, a soft little start.
In jokes whispered on breezes afloat,
A dance of goodbye, the earth's little note.

Frocks of gold flutter, like grandmas in shoes,
Kites dipped in laughter, brightening blues.
Crickets throw parties, their songs swirl and dive,
In this gentle farewell, all seem alive.

The boughs moan a tune, they swish and they sway,
Tickling the twilight, in comical play.
As shadows tumble, and dusk begins to creep,
Nature giggles softly, coaxing dreams to sleep.

So bid a fond farewell with a chuckle or two,
To the funny little moments, both old and new.
With a bow and a twirl, join the last jive,
In Nature's embrace, where laughter survives.

Secrets of the Underbrush

In the quiet grove where critters scheme,
A squirrel's got a plan, or so it would seem.
He gathers acorns, stacks them like gold,
While gossiping birds tale secrets retold.

A snail's on a journey, oh what a race!
With one foot in front, he sets a slow pace.
Laughing at rabbits that jump up and down,
He chuckles and shuffles, no need for a crown.

Much chatter occurs 'neath the tangled green,
As ants in a line form a well-oiled machine.
They carry their bounty, almost in sync,
While a worm shares a story that makes folks rethink.

A beetle struts by with a swaggering style,
Declaring himself "the king" of the mile.
The others roll eyes, it's just a good jest,
For under the leaves, they know who's the best!

Glistening Embers of Autumn

The sun sets low, paints the ground in cheer,
As pumpkins parade, with nothing to fear.
In sweaters so cozy, folks laugh and they play,
While squirrels steal snacks at the end of the day.

The chill in the air sings a tickling tune,
As leaves twirl down like a quirky festoon.
A raccoon, quite sly, plans his nighttime feast,
While critters create their own autumnal least.

The bonfire flickers, casting shadows so wide,
Where marshmallows toast on a sweet, sugary ride.
A ghost in the trees joins the laughter and song,
Chasing away worries, it won't be long!

So gather around, with your cider in hand,
As nature embraces this playful land.
For autumn's a time of hilarity bright,
Where secrets are shared in the warming light!

Nature's Daily Journals

At dawn, the robins chirp, a funny alarm,
While sleepy-eyed leaves stretch their day-long charm.
A chipmunk takes notes in a tiny, neat book,
Jotting down treasures like a well-read cook.

Each evening, the crickets put on their best show,
With a symphony grand, oh how they all glow!
A frog plays the drums, while the lilies dance,
In nature's wild concert, they all take a chance.

And nightly, the moon whispers jokes from above,
To fireflies glowing, all filled with pure love.
They wink among stars, in a bright, twinkling swirl,
Creating a story where dreams dance and twirl.

So flip through the pages of each passing day,
Where laughter and wonder are always at play.
In nature's own journal, the tales never cease,
With humor and warmth, they grant us release!

Petals in the Wind

A petal took flight on a whimsical spree,
Danced with a breeze, said, "Come twirl with me!"
It swirled past a bug with a curious stare,
Who laughed out in joy, caught up in the air.

How dandelions giggle when gusts steal their fluff,
While ants run for shelter, declaring, "Enough!"
They tumble and roll, what a sight to behold,
These petals and friends, all daring and bold.

With feathery whispers, the wind made a call,
Inviting each flower to join in the ball.
A waltz of bright colors spun round and round,
As nature chuckled, "What fun can be found!"

So here's to the blooms that take life in stride,
Who dance on a breeze, no need to hide.
For in every petal, a story is spun,
With laughter and joy, oh, isn't it fun!

Fragmented Memories of Green

In a garden of giggles, memories twine,
A cucumber slips, oh, the sun starts to shine.
The zucchini grins wide as the carrots confess,
That they're in a rush, it's a veggie mess!

Tomatoes will trot, and the beans dance a jig,
While spinach looks puzzled, it just can't be big.
The radishes chuckle, their tops all a fuss,
As the peas in their pods start a grand circus!

A cabbage rolls over, it's quite the surprise,
The broccoli's singing, oh how it can rise!
In this jolly green scene, nature's full of cheer,
With plants making jokes, and laughter so near.

So here's to the garden, where whimsies unite,
With fruit flying high, what a humorous sight!
As memories flutter, forever they'll glean,
In the patchwork of joy, where all's evergreen.

The Call of Dappled Light

Beneath branches of laughter, shadows do play,
Where squirrels hold meetings, by night and by day.
A sunflower swoons in the warmth of the glow,
While daisies giggle and twirl in a row.

The sunbeams poke fun, tossing light all around,
As mushrooms squabble, just who's underground?
With a chorus of crickets, the day bids goodbye,
While fireflies twinkle, like stars in the sky.

The brook starts to babble, with secrets to share,
Raccoons play pranks, in their furry debonair.
While owls make wisecracks, perched high on a limb,
The shadows keep chuckling, in twilight's dim whim.

So let the light dapple, let the humor take flight,
In the whispers of forests, there's joy in the night.
With laughter from creatures that flit in delight,
The call of the woodland is purely polite!

Autumn's Golden Reverie

As leaves do a tango, they flutter and swirl,
Squirrels scurry swiftly, with acorns to twirl.
The pumpkins all grin, wearing hats made of hay,
While the cider pops bubbles, in a festive display.

The apples are plotting, a rich caramel scheme,
As kids toss the gourds, oh, the laughter it seems!
The wind hums a tune that makes all creatures sway,
While farm critters gather for a grand soirée.

The geese in formation can't seem to agree,
One wants to take flight, but three want some tea!
With laughter abounding in fields painted gold,
The essence of autumn, a sight to behold.

So here's to the season, where all takes a turn,
With the winds whispering secrets, for all of us to learn.
In the rustle of colors, fun tales will unfold,
As autumn's sweet reverie warms the air, uncontrolled!

Nature's Kaleidoscope

A patch of forget-me-nots chuckles in blue,
While daisies dispute just which one is true.
The bees throw a party, with honey to share,
Each bloom brings a laugh, with fragrance in air.

The frogs on a lily pad take up the cue,
Ribbiting jokes that only they knew!
While wiggly worms wiggle in sync with the beat,
A symphony brewing with nature's own feat.

The sunflowers gossip, their heads held up high,
Did you see how the wind made my neighbor fly?
The grasshoppers leap, with a wink and a hop,
In this colorful world, where the fun never stops!

So let's take a moment, to savor the hues,
Of nature's own canvas, where laughter ensues.
With every bright petal and fluttering wing,
The kaleidoscope of life is a joyful thing!

Under the Dappled Canopy

In a park where squirrels strutted,
A sign read, 'Do not feed the nuts!'
A dance of shadows played around,
While pigeons cooed all without a sound.

The old man with his floppy hat,
Sat on a bench, patted the cat.
A child giggled, ran through the grass,
Chasing a butterfly with panache.

The sun peeked through the branches high,
Tickled the noses of passers-by.
With each rustle, the trees conspired,
Tickling the wind—a nature's choir.

Moonlight whispered late at night,
To the owls, who hooted with delight.
The trees swayed, like they were tipsy,
In a world that's far too frisky!

Garden of Echoing Days

In a garden of laughter, blooms abound,
Where daisies wear hats and dance around.
The gnomes are plotting a sneaky prank,
Watering cans full of peppermint tank.

Butterflies waltz on the breeze,
While bumblebees hum tunes with ease.
A turtle, slow, tries to break a record,
But the rabbits keep racing, so well-fed.

The old oak tree sports a grumpy face,
While shy daisies twirl without a trace.
Petunias gossip, and violets sigh,
As the sun peeks in, saying, "Oh my!"

When evening falls, the stars all wink,
Creating a scene that makes one think.
A garden alive with modern jest,
Nature's humor put to the test!

The Cycle of Sunlight and Shadow

Day breaks, the sun stretches wide,
The shadows yawn and slowly slide.
A rabbit hops as if to tease,
Chasing sunbeams with utmost ease.

The flowers giggle as bees zoom by,
In their own world, they dare to fly.
A squirrel's tumble makes everyone laugh,
As it stumbles across the sunlit path.

Evening creeps, shadows start their play,
Whispering secrets of the day.
A cat's lazy stretch, a whimsical sight,
Bringing to rest both the day and night.

With stars twinkling, a night owl calls,
Nature's laughter echoes through walls.
The cycle spins, round and round,
In a world where joy in silence is found!

Timeless Whisperings

Under the moon, the night is young,
Old trees gossip, their branches hung.
A raccoon rummages for a treat,
While fireflies chase their own little beat.

The breeze plays tricks, tickling the day,
And all the shadows dance and sway.
Laughter hides behind friendly bark,
As the sun sets with a cheery spark.

In the distance, daisies share a joke,
While the hedgehogs chuckle, what a poke!
The grasshoppers clap to a lullaby,
While crickets serenade the rosy sky.

As dawn approaches, light spills in,
Morning's laughter begins again.
Timeless whispers between the trees,
Nature chuckles—always with ease!

The Slow Descent

As I cling to my brunch, oh what a plight,
The breeze tickles gently, my dreams in flight.
A tumble, a jolt, I'm facing the ground,
With my salad in hand, I can barely be found.

A wobbly dance, I glide with a grin,
My friends all just laugh, they know where I'll spin.
With each little flap, I spiral and sway,
What a whimsical ride, come join in the play!

Through branches I zig, I zig-zag with glee,
An ungraceful dive, my fate's plain to see.
No time to be classy, etiquette lost,
I'm giving out giggles, at such merry cost!

Finally, I plop, in a crinkly heap,
My antics all done, it's time now to sleep.
With a chuckle so loud, the chaos I end,
It's all just a game—my leafy dear friend!

Cradles of Transformation

In cozy cradles, we start to decay,
Hanging out with bugs, while they dance and play.
With spots and some wrinkles, we jest and we laugh,
Who knew being crispy could be such a gaffe?

Each flicker of sunlight, a shimmer so bold,
Retelling our stories, both funny and old.
We twirl in the breeze, telling tales to the trees,
Our happy demise just sways with the leaves!

Chasing the antics of squirrels up above,
I thought I was wise, oh what do I love?
Each tumble, each frolic—a comedy role,
In nature's great show, I'm just playing my role!

With laughter and cheers, we descend toward the floor,
In a blanket of colors, we'll greet them once more.
So if you see us, bend down, have some fun,
In cradles of change, we all are still one!

Moments before the Fall

The wind starts to whisper, it's almost my time,
Should I do a flip? Oh, that would be prime!
I practice my stunts with finesse and flair,
But wobbling wildly, I've lost all my care.

How funny it seems, that I used to be green,
A vibrant young star, now I'm just a scene.
With a twist and a turn, I'm ready to start,
An acrobat's dream, as I leap with my heart!

Can I land on a pigeon? Or just on the grass?
Which way should I tumble? I hope it's first class!
My friends all are cheering, lift up for the ride,
In this comical moment, I take it in stride.

And then comes the slip, oh what a delight,
I land with a thud, in a fall of pure light.
With giggles and glee, I lay on the floor,
Moments before the tilt, I can't help but adore!

Brown Crumble and Golden Whirl

Brown crumbles beneath me, they laugh as I roll,
In a swirl of delights, I'm finding my soul.
With every spin, my joy starts to soar,
As I twirl through the air, oh give me some more!

Golden whirls, take flight, oh what a sight!
We giggle together, oh isn't this bright?
Who knew autumn could be so profound,
With adventures galore, where laughter is found?

Around and around, we dance with such flair,
Creating a ruckus, like we haven't a care.
With a chuckle and bounce, we roll side by side,
In the playful embrace, we take each wild ride.

My friends in their colors, they join in the spree,
In a world full of fun, just take it from me!
So come join the party, get ready to twirl,
In brown crumbles and gold, let laughter unfurl!

Seasons in the Wind

When autumn drapes its golden cloak,
The trees begin to dance and poke.
They shimmy, shake, and let things fly,
Oh, where'd that branch go? Oh my, oh my!

Winter comes and all looks bare,
Yet squirrels scamper with nary a care.
They hide their nuts and do a twirl,
As snowflakes join the frosty swirl.

Then spring arrives, with blooms in tow,
The croaking frogs put on a show.
They sing to birds, a cheerful match,
While sneaky ants make off with snacks.

Summer's here, the sun's a blaze,
And under shade, we all laze.
But watch your drink, those pesky bees,
They'll buzz around like they own these leaves!

Treetop Murmurs

In the trees, the chatter grows,
A parrot tells a joke that flows.
The owls giggle, the squirrels cheer,
While raccoons throw their hats in sheer.

Branches bow with a heavy creak,
"Don't blame me, it's that pesky peak!"
They share loud laughs over wrinkled bark,
As dawn gives way to light from dark.

A woodpecker taps a funny tune,
"Hey, keep it down! I'm trying to swoon!"
But the chattering leaves just won't stop,
As they share tales of their leafy flop.

The wind whips through, gives a playful shove,
"Chill out, everyone, let's fall in love!"
But the trees just giggle and sway with glee,
In their leafy world, wild and free!

Beneath the Canopy's Gaze

Underneath the leafy dome,
Lies a tale of nature's home.
The ferns chatter in windswept sighs,
While shadows play at comedic guise.

Here's a vine that's tangled tight,
"It's a game of hide and fright!"
The trees just laugh, their roots amiss,
"Join the fun; it's hard to resist!"

A caterpillar dons a dance,
Rolling in circles, taking a chance.
The beetles laugh and wave so high,
"Don't forget us, we're here to fly!"

As sunlight trickles, the scene's so bright,
Nature's jokes make everything light.
So come and listen, you'll find the thrill,
Beneath the leaves, there's laughter still!

Fading hues of Warmth

As the days start to fade away,
Colorful leaves begin their play.
A red one shouts, "Watch me spin!"
While yellow flutters with a silly grin.

"Catch me if you can!" they tease on breeze,
Twisting and turning with utmost ease.
A brown one shouts, "I'm on a roll!"
As they swirl down and fill the bowl.

In corners pile the colors bright,
While squirrels giggle in sheer delight.
"Is this a treasure? Or just old mulch?"
Fall's prankster spirit makes us lurch.

But as the chill begins to bite,
The trees tell stories into the night.
"Let's not be sad, let's laugh instead,
For fun lives on, though warmth has fled!"

The Quiet Fall

In a world of rustling cheer,
A squirrel steals my lunch near.
Chasing nuts like they're on sale,
He scurries off with a happy trail.

The ground is a crunchy carpet spread,
While I try to dodge a tree's overhead.
Branches wave like they often do,
I think they're laughing at me too.

Every flutter brings a giggle,
The trees seem to dance, wiggle and wiggle.
A leaf drops down, a clown in disguise,
I take a step back, oh how it flies!

But what fun it is to twirl and spin,
With giggling friends, let's begin!
Nature's laughter fills the scene,
As autumn tricks us, oh so keen.

Echoes in the Breeze

Whispers travel on the wind,
A joke told by the trees, grinned.
They gossip of seasons, oh so sly,
While I just sigh and let out a cry.

The breeze carries chuckles, light and free,
A cackling chorus of nature's spree.
Bouncing through branches, giggling loud,
Leaves are the jesters of the crowd.

Each rustle seems to point and tease,
As I trip over squirrels with awkward ease.
Watch out, they tease, here comes the fool,
With shoes made for dancing, oh what a rule!

Yet with each tumble and playful fall,
I laugh with the wind, answering the call.
Nature's comedians, a riotous spree,
As echoes in the breeze bring joy to me.

A Tumble of Colors

Colors tumble from up high,
A painted sky that makes me sigh.
With reds and golds in a spinning race,
I trip on my feet, but it's a lovely place.

Crisp orange landings, funny as can be,
I laugh at my shoes, they laugh back at me.
A golden gust sends a swirl round,
Dizzy now, I tumble down to the ground.

Every shade has a joke to share,
A purple leaf mocks my messy hair.
The ground, like a stage, calls out my name,
As I'm caught in the act of this silly game.

So let's color the world, let joy be our tone,
With laughter we gather, and never alone.
A tumble of colors, we dance and we play,
As autumn declares it's a comical day.

The Dance of Decay

In the midst of fading glory,
The trees tell a funny story.
Leaves drop like confetti, what a sight,
As nature hosts an autumn night.

A shuffle, a rustle, a comedic fall,
Like dancers in a quirky hall.
Twirl me around, let me spin,
As nature's show begins to begin.

Branches creak with an old man's sound,
While a nut rolls past, faster than a hound.
Trees chuckle softly, a swaying jest,
As I ponder if this is nature's best.

So let's embrace this final fling,
With laughter, the leaves do spin and swing.
In the dance of decay, we find release,
As funny tales bring us joy and peace.

Patterns of Resilience

In the garden, they tumble and fall,
Blowing past me without a call.
Each twist and turn, a little jig,
As if they're laughing, oh, what a gig!

They swirl around, a playful crew,
Attempting to hide from morning dew.
With a flip and a flap, they dance away,
Who knew they were masters of the ballet?

Underfoot, they crunch and they pop,
It's a riot, non-stop, can't make it stop!
Giggling leaves on the ground below,
Spreading cheer in this nature show!

And in the breeze, they spin and whir,
Like a tiny leaf in a whirlwind blur.
Each one a joker with tales to weave,
Who knew such fun could come from a sleeve?

Nature's Confessional.

Gather 'round, my leafy friends,
In confessions, the fun never ends!
Did you see that squirrel, so spry and bold?
He tripped right over, a sight to behold!

We laughed so hard, we nearly cried,
As he scampered off, his dignity fried.
Oh, the drama in nature, it's hard to top,
With creatures both silly, they just can't stop!

We whispered tales of the rain that poured,
How puddles turned into a slippery board.
Watch your step, it's a comedic dive,
Life's too short not to feel alive!

So here we sway, in the shade we stay,
With chuckles and giggles, we pass the day.
In this green nook, let's relish the cheer,
Nature's confessions bring laughter here!

Whispers of Autumn's Dance

Oh, the autumn, what a mischievous prank,
Leaves swirling down like a colorful tank.
They spin and they twirl, in such wild delight,
Playing tag with the winds, what a sight!

Their colors so bright, a joyous parade,
Twirling in circles, not a minute delayed.
They tease the tree with a cheeky grin,
Always saying, 'You can't catch us, win!'

With giggles and wiggles, they float through the air,
A whimsical waltz, without any care.
Rusty gold and bold orange flair,
Who knew leaves could have such fun with flair?

They whisper secrets to every passerby,
"Laugh with us now, let the worries fly!"
In this dance of delight, they sing sweetly,
Turning the mundane into something breezy!

The Tapestry of Change

Fabric of nature, a patchwork so bright,
Threaded with colors from morning to night.
Every inch tells a story, a twist of fate,
As time weaves its magic, the laughter's innate!

Oh, the squirrels with acorns, they scold and jest,
While chasing each other, they never rest.
Among the rich hues, they prance and cheer,
Creating a comedy, oh-so-dear!

In puddles of rain, they slip and glide,
With a bounce and a splash, it's a wild ride!
They say, "Join our tapestry, come have a laugh,"
As nature's own humor draws us on its path!

So watch as the seasons share giggles and glee,
The tapestry of life is wacky, you see.
With every twist and turn in the scheme,
Nature is plotting her funniest dream!

The Last Sigh of Summertime

The sun brings warmth, yet feels aloof,
A last wave goodbye from the rooftop.
The grill still smokes, with burgers galore,
While bees play tag, at the picnic's core.

A chicken struts with a jaunty gait,
While squirrels plot against the garden gate.
As bright colors fade into the night,
We laugh as the fireflies take flight.

The hammock swings with a sleepy groan,
While ice cream drips on the weathered stone.
With flip-flops on, we dance and spin,
Taking summer's farewell on the chin.

As autumn sneaks in with a rustle and chuckle,
We'll reminisce while we hug our snuggle.
But for now, let's soak up the golden rays,
In the last bright flashes of sundrenched days.

A Palette of Letting Go

Crimson drops drift through the air,
Like giggles caught in a playful stare.
The trees shed coats, all golden and bright,
While we pretend it's a dance party night.

A painter's dream with colors so bold,
Whispers of secrets and stories retold.
As branches wave, like hands in glee,
They bid farewell to their leafy spree.

Crisp crunches make our footsteps sing,
In a world where oddities take wing.
With squirrels collecting their treasure of nuts,
There's laughter echoing in our ruts.

A feathered caper, a frolicsome sight,
As nature chuckles 'neath shrinking light.
So let's twirl in the colors so free,
As we paint memories, you and me.

Murmurs of the Changing Grove

Whispers from branches swaying high,
A gossiping breeze that flutters by.
The critters gather for their morning show,
Trading tales of where the winds blow.

In leafy chatter, secrets slip,
While acorns host a nutty trip.
With every rustle, a joke in the air,
We giggle and dance, without a care.

The ground's a canvas of splattered hues,
As trees release their colorful blues.
Each step we take brings a playful crunch,
Like nature's way of throwing a brunch.

With every swirl of the autumn breeze,
Are happy confessions from buzzing bees.
In this grove where laughter grows,
Let's share the stories that nobody knows.

Treading Through Time

With each step, a crumbly crunch,
Time goes by, like a comic punch.
The calendar flips with every bat,
While we waddle through past seasons, just like that.

Nostalgia dances in hues of brown,
As we embrace the wrap of nature's gown.
With giggles echoing as we stroll the lane,
We're timeless fools with nothing to gain.

Footprints tell tales of mischief and play,
Casting shadows where we lounge and sway.
With pumpkins grinning, they cheer us on,
As we meander where memories spawn.

So let us skip through this amber maze,
With laughter lit up like a sun's warm rays.
In the cycle of change, we find our groove,
Treading through time, as we laugh and move.

Nature's Gentle Embrace

In a forest where squirrels dance with glee,
The trees gossip softly, like friends sharing tea.
A branch sways lightly, oh what a sight,
As birds chirp their secrets, feeling just right.

The flowers wear hats, oh what a delight,
While bugs form a band, playing tunes late at night.
The mossy green carpet, soft under our feet,
Makes nature's embrace just too hard to beat.

With every rustle, a giggle escapes,
As critters join in with their funny shapes.
The sunbeams burst forth, a bright golden show,
In this whimsical world, there's always a glow.

So come take a stroll, let your worries unwind,
In this silly jungle, laughter's what you'll find.
For nature's our stage, and every day's fun,
Where jokes are not scarce when you're out in the sun.

Shadows of the Canopy

Underneath the branches, shadows play tricks,
A raccoon in shades thinks he's one of the clicks.
With a wink and a grin, he snatches a snack,
While the owls roll their eyes, saying, 'Watch your back!'

The wind whispers softly, telling secrets divine,
While ants in a line march to party at nine.
The crickets chuckle, as they sing out of tune,
Creating a chaos that's over the moon.

In this jolly forest, where nonsense is king,
Every bush tells a tale, oh the joy it can bring!
From squirrels on skateboards to frogs in a band,
Nature's a circus, and it's truly well planned.

The dapples of sunlight, like laughter, they dance,
While flowers all giggle, indulging in chance.
So skip through the laughter, and wiggle your toes,
In the shadows of trees, where the funny wind blows.

The Quiet Fall

When autumn comes calling, it brings a surprise,
As leaves swirl down, like colorful flies.
The squirrels all scramble, their acorns in hand,
While the pumpkins just chuckle, 'This wasn't our plan!'

In the hush of the season, things start to sleep,
Yet the laughter of critters wakes not from deep.
With a rustle and tumble, a maple leaf rolls,
And the chipmunks just giggle, counting their goals.

The chill in the air, it plays hide and seek,
While coyotes howl softly, like they're on a streak.
The wind tells a joke as it swirls through the trees,
Tickling all the branches, just trying to tease.

So gather 'round gently, as the days grow cold,
In this comic landscape, watch stories unfold.
With laughter and light, the world's far from dreary,
In autumn's embrace, the mood's just too cheery.

A Symphony of Green and Gold

In the heart of the woods, a band starts to play,
With frogs on the drums and birds leading the sway.
The vines are the strings, gently strumming along,
While butterflies flutter, harmonizing the song.

The wind is a maestro, conducting the show,
As the grasses all sway, putting on quite the glow.
Each leaf plays a note in this natural spree,
Creating a melody that sets spirits free.

The flowers burst forth, bursting with cheer,
As bees hum along, buzzing loud and clear.
What a symphony bright, in colors so bold,
A circus of life, where no tale goes untold.

So dance in the rhythm, let nature take lead,
In this whimsical concert, our laughter's the seed.
With each twirl and spin, let the fun overflow,
In this harmony pure, where the good vibes will flow.

Nature's Mosaic

In the garden, colors clash,
Flowers gossip, making a splash.
Bees wear sunglasses, bright and bold,
While worms tell secrets, never old.

Sunlight winks, painting the scene,
A squirrel's dance, quite routine.
Frogs in tuxedos, ready to prance,
Nature knows how to throw a dance!

Rabbits hop in stylish attire,
Chasing shadows, never tire.
Butterflies flaunt their patterned wings,
In this world, hilarity sings.

So come join the fun, don't be shy,
With every step, the giggles fly.
Nature's mosaic, laughter unbound,
Brighten your day, joy all around.

Shadows on the Ground

Walking through the park on a sunny day,
I step on shadows that dance and sway.
They wiggle and jiggle, what a funny sight,
Chasing my feet, ready to bite!

Trees play hide and seek in the light,
Their branches stretch far, what a delight!
A breeze whispers jokes, laughter's the goal,
As shadows giggle, they're taking a toll!

Silly old sun, he tickles the ground,
Painting stories in shadows all around.
"Catch me if you can!" they tease with glee,
Every step I take is a folly of spree.

So I leap and I bound, join the parade,
Where shadows and laughter are never delayed.
In this quirky dance, joy knows no end,
With shadows as company, oh, what a trend!

Pages of the Earth

Turn the pages of the grassy field,
Where laughter spills and joy is revealed.
Every flower, a laugh, every tree, a quip,
Nature's own book; come take a trip!

The bees are authors, buzzing their tunes,
Writing bestsellers 'neath bright afternoon moons.
Frogs leap in comic strips, tails in the air,
While critters converse, without a care!

Squirrels pen stories with acorns and twigs,
Making mischief, pulling off gigs.
And if you listen, you might just hear,
The chorus of nature, oh, how they cheer!

So let's flip the pages, embrace all the fun,
In this wild library, under the sun.
With laughter as ink and joy as the pen,
A magical story again and again!

Unfolding Stories

Every petal tells a tale, bright and spry,
As butterflies flutter in a joyous high.
Grass blades whisper secrets in silly tones,
Nature unfolds her stories; they're never alone!

Caterpillars in ruffles, on a grand spree,
Practicing ballet, just wait and see!
Beetles debate who's the best dancer,
In this lively world, there's always a prancer!

Hiccups of laughter ring through the trees,
A symphony played by the buzzing bees.
Sticks and stones, they're plotting a play,
What roles they'll take, who knows today?

So bet on the branches, dive into the groove,
With every moment, there's room to move.
Unfolding stories in colors and sound,
In this cheerful dance, pure happiness found!

www.ingramcontent.com/pod-product-compliance
Lightning Source LLC
Chambersburg PA
CBHW070319120526
44590CB00017B/2740